HAL•LEONARD

INSTRUMENTAL
PLAY-ALONG

AUDIO
ACCESS
INCLUDED

PLAYBACK+
Speed • Pitch • Balance • Loop

HORN

JAZZ BLUES FAVORITES

T0070691

Audio arrangements by Peter Deneff

To access audio visit:
www.halleonard.com/mylibrary

Enter Code
5593-9304-6602-0611

ISBN 978-1-4950-5341-2

HAL•LEONARD®

7777 W. BLUEMOUND RD. P.O. BOX 13819 MILWAUKEE, WI 53213

Visit Hal Leonard Online at
www.halleonard.com

ALL BLUES

Horn

By MILES DAVIS

BASIN STREET BLUES

Horn

Words and Music by
SPENCER WILLIAMS

BIRK'S WORKS

Horn

By DIZZY GILLESPIE

C-JAM BLUES

Horn

By DUKE ELLINGTON

FREDDIE FREELOADER

Horn

By MILES DAVIS

MR. P.C.

Horn

By JOHN COLTRANE

NIGHT TRAIN

Horn

Words by OSCAR WASHINGTON
and LEWIS C. SIMPKINS
Music by JIMMY FORREST

NOW'S THE TIME

Horn

By CHARLIE PARKER

ONE FOR DADDY-O

Horn

By NAT ADDERLY

THE SWINGIN' SHEPHERD BLUES

HORN

Words and Music by MOE KOFFMAN,
RHODA ROBERTS and KENNY JACOBSON

TENOR MADNESS

Horn

By SONNY ROLLINS

THINGS AIN'T WHAT THEY USED TO BE

HORN

By MERCER ELLINGTON

Your favorite songs are arranged just for solo instrumentalists with this outstanding series. Each book includes a great full-accompaniment play-along audio so you can sound just like a pro! Check out www.halleonard.com to see all the titles available.

Chart Hits

All About That Bass • All of Me • Happy • Radioactive • Roar • Say Something • Shake It Off • A Sky Full of Stars • Someone like You • Stay with Me • Thinking Out Loud • Uptown Funk.

00146207	Flute	$12.99
00146208	Clarinet	$12.99
00146209	Alto Sax	$12.99
00146210	Tenor Sax	$12.99
00146211	Trumpet	$12.99
00146212	Horn	$12.99
00146213	Trombone	$12.99
00146214	Violin	$12.99
00146215	Viola	$12.99
00146216	Cello	$12.99

Coldplay

Clocks • Every Teardrop Is a Waterfall • Fix You • In My Place • Lost! • Paradise • The Scientist • Speed of Sound • Trouble • Violet Hill • Viva La Vida • Yellow.

00103337	Flute	$12.99
00103338	Clarinet	$12.99
00103339	Alto Sax	$12.99
00103340	Tenor Sax	$12.99
00103341	Trumpet	$12.99
00103342	Horn	$12.99
00103343	Trombone	$12.99
00103344	Violin	$12.99
00103345	Viola	$12.99
00103346	Cello	$12.99

Disney Greats

Arabian Nights • Hawaiian Roller Coaster Ride • It's a Small World • Look Through My Eyes • Yo Ho (A Pirate's Life for Me) • and more.

00841934	Flute	$12.99
00841935	Clarinet	$12.99
00841936	Alto Sax	$12.99
00841937	Tenor Sax	$12.95
00841938	Trumpet	$12.99
00841939	Horn	$12.95
00841940	Trombone	$12.95
00841941	Violin	$12.99
00841942	Viola	$12.95
00841943	Cello	$12.99
00842078	Oboe	$12.99

Great Themes

Bella's Lullaby • Chariots of Fire • Get Smart • Hawaii Five-O Theme • I Love Lucy • The Odd Couple • Spanish Flea • and more.

00842468	Flute	$12.99
00842469	Clarinet	$12.99
00842470	Alto Sax	$12.99
00842471	Tenor Sax	$12.99
00842472	Trumpet	$12.99
00842473	Horn	$12.99
00842474	Trombone	$12.99
00842475	Violin	$12.99
00842476	Viola	$12.99
00842477	Cello	$12.99

Lennon & McCartney Favorites

All You Need Is Love • A Hard Day's Night • Here, There and Everywhere • Hey Jude • Let It Be • Nowhere Man • Penny Lane • She Loves You • When I'm Sixty-Four • and more.

00842600	Flute	$12.99
00842601	Clarinet	$12.99
00842603	Tenor Sax	$12.99
00842604	Trumpet	$12.99
00842605	Horn	$12.99
00842607	Violin	$12.99
00842608	Viola	$12.99
00842609	Cello	$12.99

Popular Hits

Breakeven • Fireflies • Halo • Hey, Soul Sister • I Gotta Feeling • I'm Yours • Need You Now • Poker Face • Viva La Vida • You Belong with Me • and more.

00842511	Flute	$12.99
00842512	Clarinet	$12.99
00842513	Alto Sax	$12.99
00842514	Tenor Sax	$12.99
00842515	Trumpet	$12.99
00842516	Horn	$12.99
00842517	Trombone	$12.99
00842518	Violin	$12.99
00842519	Viola	$12.99
00842520	Cello	$12.99

Songs from Frozen, Tangled and Enchanted

Do You Want to Build a Snowman? • For the First Time in Forever • Happy Working Song • I See the Light • In Summer • Let It Go • Mother Knows Best • That's How You Know • True Love's First Kiss • When Will My Life Begin • and more.

00126921	Flute	$14.99
00126922	Clarinet	$14.99
00126923	Alto Sax	$14.99
00126924	Tenor Sax	$14.99
00126925	Trumpet	$14.99
00126926	Horn	$14.99
00126927	Trombone	$14.99
00126928	Violin	$14.99
00126929	Viola	$14.99
00126930	Cello	$14.99

Top Hits

Adventure of a Lifetime • Budapest • Die a Happy Man • Ex's & Oh's • Fight Song • Hello • Let It Go • Love Yourself • One Call Away • Pillowtalk • Stitches • Writing's on the Wall.

00171073	Flute	$12.99
00171074	Clarinet	$12.99
00171075	Alto Sax	$12.99
00171106	Tenor Sax	$12.99
00171107	Trumpet	$12.99
00171108	Horn	$12.99
00171109	Trombone	$12.99
00171110	Violin	$12.99
00171111	Viola	$12.99
00171112	Cello	$12.99

Wicked

As Long As You're Mine • Dancing Through Life • Defying Gravity • For Good • I'm Not That Girl • Popular • The Wizard and I • and more.

00842236	Flute	$12.99
00842237	Clarinet	$11.99
00842238	Alto Saxophone	$11.95
00842239	Tenor Saxophone	$11.95
00842240	Trumpet	$11.99
00842241	Horn	$11.95
00842242	Trombone	$12.99
00842243	Violin	$11.99
00842244	Viola	$12.99
00842245	Cello	$12.99

HAL•LEONARD®

101 SONGS

YOUR FAVORITE SONGS ARE ARRANGED FOR SOLO INSTRUMENTALISTS WITH THIS GREAT SERIES.

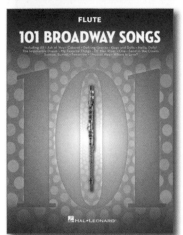

101 BROADWAY SONGS

Cabaret • Do You Hear the People Sing? • Edelweiss • Guys and Dolls • Hello, Dolly! • I Dreamed a Dream • If I Were a Bell • Luck Be a Lady • Ol' Man River • Seasons of Love • Send in the Clowns • Think of Me • Tomorrow • What I Did for Love • and many more.

00154199	Flute	$14.99
00154200	Clarinet	$14.99
00154201	Alto Sax	$14.99
00154202	Tenor Sax	$14.99
00154203	Trumpet	$14.99
00154204	Horn	$14.99
00154205	Trombone	$14.99
00154206	Violin	$14.99
00154207	Viola	$14.99
00154208	Cello	$14.99

101 HIT SONGS

All About That Bass • All of Me • Brave • Breakaway • Clocks • Fields of Gold • Firework • Hey, Soul Sister • Ho Hey • I Gotta Feeling • Jar of Hearts • Love Story • 100 Years • Roar • Rolling in the Deep • Shake It Off • Smells like Teen Spirit • Uptown Funk • and more.

00194561	Flute	$16.99
00197182	Clarinet	$16.99
00197183	Alto Sax	$16.99
00197184	Tenor Sax	$16.99
00197185	Trumpet	$16.99
00197186	Horn	$16.99
00197187	Trombone	$16.99
00197188	Violin	$16.99
00197189	Viola	$16.99
00197190	Cello	$16.99

101 CLASSICAL THEMES

Ave Maria • Bist du bei mir (You Are with Me) • Canon in D • Clair de Lune • Dance of the Sugar Plum Fairy • 1812 Overture • Eine Kleine Nachtmusik ("Serenade"), First Movement Excerpt • The Flight of the Bumble Bee • Funeral March of a Marionette • Fur Elise • Gymnopedie No. 1 • Jesu, Joy of Man's Desiring • Lullaby • Minuet in G • Ode to Joy • Piano Sonata in C • Pie Jesu • Rondeau • Theme from Swan Lake • Wedding March • William Tell Overture • and many more.

00155315	Flute	$14.99
00155317	Clarinet	$14.99
00155318	Alto Sax	$14.99
00155319	Tenor Sax	$14.99
00155320	Trumpet	$14.99
00155321	Horn	$14.99
00155322	Trombone	$14.99
00155323	Violin	$14.99
00155324	Viola	$14.99
00155325	Cello	$14.99

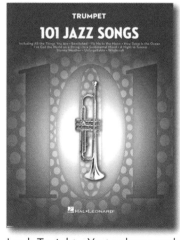

101 JAZZ SONGS

All of Me • Autumn Leaves • Bewitched • Blue Skies • Body and Soul • Cheek to Cheek • Come Rain or Come Shine • Don't Get Around Much Anymore • A Fine Romance • Here's to Life • I Could Write a Book • It Could Happen to You • The Lady Is a Tramp • Like Someone in Love • Lullaby of Birdland • The Nearness of You • On Green Dolphin Street • Satin Doll • Stella by Starlight • Tangerine • Unforgettable • The Way You Look Tonight • Yesterdays • and many more.

00146363	Flute	$14.99
00146364	Clarinet	$14.99
00146366	Alto Sax	$14.99
00146367	Tenor Sax	$14.99
00146368	Trumpet	$14.99
00146369	Horn	$14.99
00146370	Trombone	$14.99
00146371	Violin	$14.99
00146372	Viola	$14.99
00146373	Cello	$14.99

HAL•LEONARD®

www.halleonard.com

Prices, contents and availability subject to change without notice.

O217